THE
FROG PRINCE
DRINKS
DIET CROAK

AND
OTHER WACKY
FAIRY TALE JOKES

PRINCELY RIDDLES

What's a frog prince's favorite candy?

A lollihop.

Why did the frog prince go out with a prune?

He couldn't get a date.

What does a chubby frog prince drink?

Diet Croak.

POPPA BEAR SCARE

What do you call a 500-pound Poppa Bear with a short temper?

"Sir!"

Where does Poppa Bear sit on an airplane?

Anywhere he wants to!

BEAR-LY FUNNY

Which hand did Goldilocks use to stir her porridge?

Neither hand — she used a spoon!

Which fairy tale do little monsters like best?

"Ghoul-dilocks and the Three Scares."

PINOCCHI-HO HO!

Knock, knock!
Who's there?
Chimney.
Chimney who?
Chimney cricket!

Why didn't Pinocchio want to go to school?

He was afraid of the spelling bee!

SNOW WHAT?

What's Snow White's brother's name?

Egg White! Get the yolk?

What should Snow White do if she finds a blue poisoned apple?

Cheer it up!

What did the prince think of Snow White?

He thought she was a little flaky.

PEEP! PEEP!

Where does Bo Peep take her sheep for their haircuts?

To the baa-baa shop!

What would you get if you crossed a shepherdess with a stick of bubble gum?

Little Bo Pop!

SHORT RIDDLES

What game do the Seven Dwarfs like to play?

Mine-opoly.

Knock, knock.
Who's there?
Hi.
Hi who?
Hi who? Hi ho! It's off to work we go!

BEWITCHED!

What does a wicked witch like to read in the newspaper?

Her horror scope!

What's worse than being a 300-pound witch with six fat black cats?

Being her broom!

Which witches like to play croquet?

Wicket witches!

FIRE-BREATHING RIDDLES

Why do dragons sleep all day?

So they can fight knights.

What's bigger than a dragon but lighter than a feather?

A dragon's shadow.

What was the dragon doing on the highway?

About fifty miles an hour.

A WITTY KITTY

What do you get when you cross a cat and a pair of galoshes?

Puss in Boots.

When is it bad luck to have Puss in Boots cross your path?

When you're a mouse.

RIDDLES IN SHINING ARMOR

What kind of fish do knights like to catch?

Swordfish.

What's the most dangerous time for a knight?

Knightfall.

Where did the knight take his sick steed?

To the horsepital.

CHECK-I

PIGGY RIDDLES

Why did the swineherd name the new pig "Ink"?

Because he kept running out of the pen.

How is getting up at dawn like a pig's tail?

It's twirly (too early).

HAVE A BALL!

Why was Cinderella such a lousy baseball player?

She had a pumpkin for a coach.

Why did Cinderella get kicked off the baseball team?

She always ran away from the ball.

WANDA WHY THESE ARE FUNNY?

What does a fairy godmother say when she does her laundry?

"Wishy-washy!"

How does a fairy godmother like her wash to come out?

Snow white.

What kind of clothes does a fairy godmother like best?

Wish 'n' wear!

BEASTLY RIDDLES

How could Beauty stop the Beast from smelling?

Hold his nose!

How does the Beast count to twenty-seven?

On his fingers.

HANSEL'S HA-HAS

Why didn't Gretel feel like dropping little bits of bread crumbs?

It was a crummy job.

What kind of cookie did the old witch give Hansel?

A misfortune cookie!

How many gingerbread cookies could Hansel
eat on an empty stomach?

*Just one — after that his stomach wasn't
empty!*

GIANT RIDDLES

On which side of the giant's house does the beanstalk grow?

On the outside!

Why was the baby giant punished for chasing Jack around the cottage?

She wasn't supposed to play with her food.

How does Jack know when the beans are ripe?

Jack and the beans talk.

ONCE A POND A TIME

What happened to the frog prince's carriage when he parked in a NO PARKING zone?

It got toad away.

Where does a frog prince go to change his clothes?

Into the croakroom.

What do you call a frog prince who rides first class on an airplane?

A passenger.

MORE CINDERIDDLES

What did Cinderella say when her photographs weren't ready?

"Some day my prints will come!"

What does Cinderella wear when she goes to the beach?

Glass flippers.

SCAT!

Which fairy tale hero has eight legs and lives under the sea?

Octo-Puss in Boots.

What does Puss in Boots say when he stubs his toe?

"Meowch!"

ICE COLD RIDDLES

What did the Snow Queen have for lunch?

An iceburger.

Why can't the Snow Queen get married?

'Cause there's No Snowking allowed.

FLAKY RIDDLES

Where does the Snow Queen keep her money?

In a snow bank.

How does the Snow Queen make her bed?

With a sheet of ice.

BO-HOO!

What would you get if you crossed a
shepherdess and a sheep dog?

Little Bo Pup.

What would you get if you crossed a
shepherdess and a honking car?

Little Bo Beep!

What if you crossed a shepherdess and a ghost?

Little Boo Peep!

EVEN BEASTLIER RIDDLES

Why did the Beast's mother knit the Beast
three socks?

Because she heard he had grown another foot.

What time was it when the ten Beasts started
chasing Beauty?

Ten after one.

SOME VERY SWINE RIDDLES

What did the swineherd call the thief who stole his pigs?

A hamburglar.

What did the swineherd give his sick pig?

Oinkment.

FAIRY TALE BOOKS YOU'LL NEVER READ

Jack Climbs the Beanstalk
   by Willie Makeit

Why Cinderella Walked Home From the Ball
   by Misty Bus

I Danced With the Prince All Night
   by Bella D. Ball

EVEN BIGGER!

Why were the giant's fingers only eleven inches long?

> *Because if they were twelve inches long, they'd be a foot!*

What did one of the giant's eyes say to the other?

> *Just between us, something smells.*

JACK 'N' JILL

Jill: Are you having a nice summer?
Jack: Yes, but I had a terrible fall.

When should Jack and Jill say no thanks to spaghetti sauce?

When it's cooked by the saucerer's apprentice.

A BAD SPELL OF RIDDLES

Would you rather a wicked witch was after you, or a giant?

I'd rather the witch was after the giant!

How does a wicked witch cross the ocean?

In a witch craft.

ZZZZZZZZZ!

What do you say to Sleeping Beauty?

Say anything you want to — she can't hear you!

Why should you never believe Sleeping Beauty?

Because she's lying.

What flowers grew under Sleeping Beauty's nose?

Two lips (tulips).

QUACKY RIDDLES

Why couldn't the Ugly Duckling fly upside down?

He was afraid he'd quack up!

Why did the Ugly Duckling cross the road?

He was filling in for the chicken.

What would you get if you crossed the Ugly Duckling with a cow?

Milk and quackers.

RIDDLES TO TICKLE YOUR ELF!

What kind of leather do elves say make the best shoes?

Who knows? But banana peels make the best slippers!

What do you call a dozen elves?

Tw-elves.

How do elves learn to read?

First they learn the elfabet.

FROGGIE FUNNIES

What happens when a frog prince falls into the pond?

He gets wet.

What do frog princes like to eat with their hamburgers?

French flies.

Where do frog princes fly their flags?

On tadpoles.

ROBBIN' ROBIN

What's green and has a runny nose?

Robin Hood with a cold.

Why did Robin Hood rob the rich?

Because the poor didn't have any money!

LITTLE BO RIDDLES

What did Little Bo Peep say to her sheep?

"I love ewe."

What would you get if you crossed Bo Peep's littlest sheep with a karate expert?

Lamb chops.

EVEN FLAKIER

Why couldn't the Snow Queen keep a secret?
Because her teeth were always chattering.

Where does the Snow Queen go to dance?
To the snow ball.

What would you get if you crossed the Snow Queen with a vampire?

Frostbite!

PEA IS FOR PRINCESS

Why did the princess go to bed?

Because the bed wouldn't come to her!

Which princess is the tallest one?

The one that lies longest in bed.

MORE FAIRY TALES YOU'LL NEVER READ

Did the Three Little Pigs Really Win?
  by Howard I. Noh

Into the Haunted Forest
  by Hugo First

The Night the Prince's Pants Fell Down
  by Lucy Lastic

The King Who Couldn't Sleep
  by Eliza Wake

BIG BAD RIDDLES

What's the difference between a big bad wolf and a flea?

A wolf can have fleas, but a flea can't have wolves!

What's the best way to talk to the big bad wolf?

Long distance!

THIS LITTLE PIGGY

Which little pig ate the most food?

The piggest one!

Why was the first little pig helping the old wolf across the street?

Because he was a Cub Snout.

HERE'S THAT CAT!

Does Puss in Boots like to eat hot dogs?

Yes, with plenty of mouse*tard!*

Why did Puss in Boots let the genie out of the bottle?

He was hoping to be granted three fishes.

Why did Puss in Boots get a raise?

He always did a mice job.

How did Puss in Boots find his way around?

With a road-ent (rodent) map.

Where does Puss in Boots like to march?

In a purrade.

What fairy tale hero is furry and joined the navy?

Puss in Boats.

CURSES ON THESE RIDDLES!

How does a wicked witch on a broomstick drink her tea?

From a flying saucer!

Why was the wicked witch packing her suitcase?

She was going away for a spell.

SNOW WHITE'S FUNNY FRIENDS

The Seven Dwarfs were huddled together under one little umbrella, but none of them got wet. How come?

It wasn't raining.

Where did the prince learn to be so charming?

He went to charm school!

MOTHER HUBBARD LAUGHS IT UP

What happened when Old Mother Hubbard fed her dog an onion?

His bark was worse than his bite!

What did Old Mother Hubbard's dog like to eat for breakfast?

Pooched eggs and barkon.

CASTLE CACKLES

Spirit: May I come in and haunt your castle?
Queen: Certainly! Be my ghost!

Queen: Is it true that a giant won't hurt you if you carry a torch?
King: It depends on how fast you carry it!

What is a kingdom?

A *stupid king.*

Why couldn't the princess's pony talk?

It was a little hoarse.

What game do knights' horses like to play?

Stable tennis.

THE END OF THE WICKED WITCHES

What do you call a nervous wicked witch?

A twitch.

How does the wicked witch keep her hair in place?

With scare spray!

Why are the wicked witch twins so confusing?

Because it's hard to tell which witch is which.

GIANT-IC!

What kind of beans do giants like to eat?
Human beans (beings)!

What should Jack take when he sees a giant?
Giant steps!

Why did the giant wear red suspenders?
To keep his pants up.

What time was it when Jack saw the giant?

Time to run!